GLACIERS

Edited by Colin Baxter Photography
Designed by Colin Baxter Photography
Printed in China

01   02   03   04   05   5   4   3   2   1

Library of Congress Cataloging-in-Publication Data
Gordon, J. E. (John E.)
Glaciers / text by John Gordon.
p. cm. -- (Worldlife library)
Includes bibliographical references (p. 72).
Summary: Introduces the formation, flow, changing nature, and effects of glaciers.
ISBN 0-89658-559-X
1. Glaciers--Juvenile literature. [1. Glaciers.] 1. Title. II. World life library.
GB2403.8 .G67 2001
551.31'2--dc21
2001026862

Distributed in Canada by Raincoast Books, 9050 Shaughnessy Street, Vancouver, B.C. V6P 6E5
Published by Voyageur Press, Inc.
123 North Second Street, P.O. Box 338, Stillwater, MN 55082 U.S.A.
651-430-2210, fax 651-430-2211
books@voyageurpress.com   www.voyageurpress.com

Educators, fundraisers, premium and gift buyers, publicists, and marketing managers:
Looking for creative products and new sales ideas? Voyageur Press books are available at special discounts when purchased in quantities, and special editions can be created to your specifications. For details contact the marketing department at 800-888-9653.

Photographs copyright © 2001 by

GLACIERS

John Ewart Gordon

WORLDLIFE
LIBRARY

Voyageur Press

Mountain icefield and subpolar glaciers, Ellesmere Island, Canada.

Contents

Introduction

*Nature chose for a tool not the earthquake or lightning to rend and split asunder,
nor the strong torrent nor eroding rain, but the tender snowflakes, falling
through unnumbered centuries, the offspring of sun and sea.*

John Muir, *Mountains of California*, 1894.

Glaciers are among the most majestic of nature's wonders. They are a source of great fascination and challenge, drawing tourists, scientists and mountaineers to their icy realms – tourists to admire from a distance the wonders of alpine scenery or the spectacle of ice cliffs crashing into the sea; scientists to decipher the history of past climates and to learn possible lessons for the future, and mountaineers to explore the frozen wilderness.

Glaciers are dynamic bodies of ice that grow and shrink with the changing climate. Several times in the recent geological past, glaciers have expanded to cover large areas of North America and Europe. As little as 20,000 years ago, cities such as New York, Chicago, Oslo and Stockholm, if they had existed, would have lain frozen below a blanket of ice hundreds of meters thick. This same ice shaped many of our landscapes and natural landmarks – among them the basins now occupied by the Great Lakes, the fjords of Norway and Alaska, the glens of Scotland and Yosemite Valley.

Not only are glaciers powerful shapers of the landscape, they are also wonderful natural laboratories. Their hidden depths contain a history of the Earth's climate, just like the annual rings of a tree, but over a much longer time period. The story the ice sheets tell is one of rapid and regular changes between global cooling and global warming.

Today we are still in the ice age, although in a brief, warmer interlude. Glaciers are

The calving front of Alsek Glacier discharges small icebergs into Alsek Lake, St Elias Mountains, Alaska.

now confined to the polar regions and higher mountains. They cover approximately ten percent of the world's land surface; most of this is found beneath the great ice sheets of Antarctica and Greenland. The volume of water contained in the world's glaciers is equivalent to a sea level rise of about 213 feet (65 meters), enough to drown large parts of Florida and the eastern seaboard of the United States, as well as other low-lying countries. Fortunately, collapse of the big ice sheets is unlikely in the foreseeable future, although continued global warming will result in the disappearance of smaller mountain glaciers, most of which are in retreat throughout the world.

The tidewater Turner Glacier, Disenchantment Bay, Alaska.

This book outlines many different facets of glaciers including: how they form and flow, how they shape the landscape, how they record climate changes and how they are responding to global warming. It reveals the existence of large lakes underneath the ice sheet in Antarctica, glaciers that suddenly flow at speeds up to a hundred times their normal rate, disintegrating ice shelves and catastrophic glacial floods.

Ice pinnacles, Hole in the Wall Glacier, Alaska.

From Tender Snowflakes to Mighty Glaciers

How Glaciers Form

Glaciers form and grow through the accumulation of snow and ice. Where the amount of snowfall in winter exceeds the loss by melting in summer, the snow accumulates from year to year, and over time the delicate snow crystals are transformed into ice. This may take only a few years in the coastal mountains of Alaska, but over a thousand years in the coldest parts of Antarctica. The highest rates of accumulation occur in maritime mountain areas; the lowest in polar and continental areas such as Antarctica and central Asia. Loss of snow and ice from glaciers, known as 'ablation', principally occurs through melting in their lower reaches. Most glaciers have a well defined 'accumulation area' in their upper reaches and an 'ablation area' in their lower reaches. The existence of glaciers, therefore, reflects the balance between accumulation and ablation. The nature of this balance is a measure of their 'state of health'. Where it is positive over a period of time (more snow and ice being added each year than is lost through ablation), the glaciers are healthy and growing; where it is negative (more ice being lost by ablation than is added each year), the glaciers shrink.

Glaciers exist in many parts of the world today, both in maritime areas (such as southeast Alaska) where there are high rates of accumulation and melting, and in polar and continental areas where although the snowfall is minimal, melting is also very low because of the low temperatures. In the center of Antarctica, for example, snow accumulation is minimal, but the ice sheet exists because there is very little melting. Reflecting these climatic factors, the altitudes at which glaciers occur generally increase from sea level in the polar areas to around 13,000-16,500 feet (4000-5000 meters) at the Equator on the volcanoes and other high mountains of the Andes, Africa and New Guinea. Where glaciers end in the sea, masses of ice break off in a process known as 'calving'. The resulting icebergs then float away at

The heavily crevassed Fjallsjökull descends steeply from the Vatnajökull ice cap, Iceland.

the mercy of the ocean currents. Calving of icebergs forms a large part of the annual loss of ice from Antarctica.

Ice on the Move

As a mass of snow and ice accumulates on the side of a mountain, it begins to flow and spread out under its own weight – a glacier is born. Glaciers flow slowly through plastic deformation of the ice. If the strength of the ice is exceeded, the ice fractures. This is evident in the spectacular crevasses on steep or fast-flowing glaciers. Although they might appear bottomless and able to swallow up unwary mountaineers, particularly when concealed by snow bridges, crevasses in glaciers outside the polar regions generally do not exceed about 100 feet (30 meters) in depth; below this depth the plastic flow of the ice closes them.

Some glaciers flow by sliding over their beds, as well as by internal plastic deformation. It may seem strange, but water can exist at the bottom of glaciers, melted by heat flow from within the Earth. Such glaciers are described as 'warm-based'. The water exists as a very thin layer and provides lubrication that helps the glaciers to slide over the underlying bedrock surface. As the glaciers slide, this creates more friction, which generates more heat and, hence, more melting. Sometimes glaciers flow over a layer of unfrozen sediment (usually a mixture of stones, clay and silt known as 'till') rather than directly on the bedrock. Where there is a lot of water present, the resulting slurry acts as a 'deformable bed' that provides additional lubrication for glacier sliding. Generally, glaciers in maritime areas have water at their beds and move by sliding at speeds up to several hundred feet or more per year. In polar and continental areas, glaciers are more often frozen to their beds and move very slowly at only a few feet or tens of feet per year. Such glaciers are described as 'cold-based'. However, some parts of the polar ice sheets, known as 'ice streams', have water and deformable sediments at their beds and flow relatively fast at speeds of one to two miles per year.

Every so often, some glaciers accelerate rapidly, or 'surge', at speeds up to 100 times their normal rate. For example, Variegated Glacier, in Alaska, exceeded speeds of 130 feet (40 meters) per day during a surge in 1982/83. During a surge, the normal meltwater

A chaotic world of collapsing ice pinnacles, South Sawyer Glacier, Alaska.

drainage under the glacier becomes blocked. Water builds up, lubricating the bed and any sediment present, allowing the glacier to accelerate. As the surge moves down the glacier, the surface of the ice becomes heavily crevassed. Surges may result in glacier fronts advancing several miles in a few months, sometimes pushing up large moraines (accumulations of rock debris) in front of them. A surge may last from a few months to a few years, before the glacier reverts to normal flow. Periods between surges may last for several decades.

Numerous examples of surge-type glaciers occur in Alaska, Iceland and Svalbard and they are often recognizable by the presence of contorted moraines on their surfaces. Some of the most spectacular surges have been reported from the Karakoram Mountains in Pakistan, where, in 1953, Kutiah Glacier advanced nearly 7½ miles (12 kilometers) in two months. Surges typically occur in remote mountain areas and rarely represent a hazard. However, in four months, between December 1936 and March 1937, the occupants of the Rapids Roadhouse on the Richardson Highway in Alaska watched as the Black Rapids Glacier advanced 3.7 miles (6 kilometers) across the Delta River valley. Fortunately, the surge stopped short of the highway and the roadhouse. The Trans-Alaska Oil Pipeline now runs alongside the highway, but a future surge of the glacier is not believed to be a significant threat.

Ice-scoured bedrock with striations, Canada.

Glaciers at Work

Glaciers modify the landscape through processes of erosion and deposition. Warm-based glaciers are particularly effective. Rock particles embedded in the glacier sole act like sandpaper on the underlying bedrock, grinding the surface down slowly over time. The effects are seen as scratches or 'striations' scored into the rock, which are orientated in the direction of ice flow. Glaciers can also exert even more powerful forces capable of crushing and fracturing the bedrock. The weakened rock is then 'plucked' or 'quarried' from the bed by the moving ice and transported away. It is later deposited underneath the glacier or dumped in moraines at the glacier terminus.

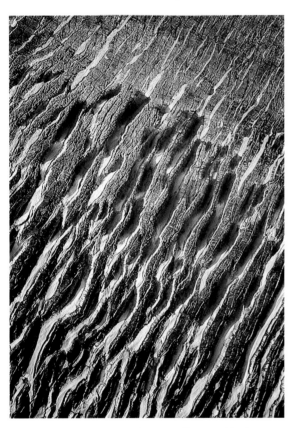

Crevasse pattern, Bering Glacier, Alaska.

During transport, some rock particles are crushed further as they come into contact with each other and the bedrock beneath. The pulverized rock produces a fine 'rock flour'. Where this is washed out in suspension by glacial rivers, it gives the water a characteristic 'milky' appearance.

Water is an integral part of most glaciers. It is produced by melting of snow and ice at the surface, by rainfall in summer and by melting at the bed. Some meltwater runs straight off the glacier surface. Some finds its way deep into the glacier in crevasses and vertical shafts known as 'moulins'. The powerful torrents that emerge at the icefront spread out across the area in front of the glacier, known as an 'outwash plain'. They deposit sand and gravel carried from the bed of the glacier and re-shape the ground in front of it.

In contrast, where glaciers are frozen to their beds, they are normally ineffective agents of erosion, so that the pre-existing land surface is sometimes preserved. Such landscapes occur in parts of the Canadian Arctic, Labrador, northern Scandinavia and northeast Scotland.

Glaciers and Climate

Glaciers generally advance when the climate gets colder or the amount of snowfall

*A nunatak breaks the smooth surface outlines of the Vatnajökull ice cap,
Iceland. In the foreground, meltwater has collected in a small surface pond.*

increases, so that more ice is delivered to the front than is melted. They retreat when the climate gets warmer or snowfall decreases. However, there is usually a time delay between changes in accumulation and ablation and changes in the position of the glacier front. Small valley glaciers respond relatively rapidly to climate changes and will usually reflect short-term changes in climate over a decade or so. Large valley glaciers take longer to respond and their behavior reflects changes in climate over several decades. Therefore, different glaciers in the same area may behave differently to short-term changes in climate, but ultimately they will respond similarly to longer-term changes. Ice sheets respond much more slowly; for example, parts of the Antarctic ice sheet may still be responding to climate warming that occurred thousands of years ago.

Some glaciers are very responsive. For example, Franz Josef Glacier on the west coast of New Zealand was generally retreating from the late nineteenth century until 1982. Since then, it has advanced by over a kilometer, in contrast to most New Zealand glaciers, which have continued to retreat slowly. The behavior of the Franz Josef Glacier reflects the high snowfall it receives and its steep narrow course, so that any changes are rapidly amplified in the response of the glacier front.

Tasman Glacier, Southern Alps, New Zealand.

Glaciers that calve into the sea ('tidewater' glaciers) or lakes are particularly notable for their variable patterns of behavior, which can involve rapid advances and retreats between stable positions. As well as climate, their behavior also depends on factors such as water depth and the position of anchoring

The heavily crevassed surface of Hubbard Glacier, Alaska.

points. Typically, they advance into the sea or lakes by pushing a moraine shoal in front, which helps to stabilize them. However, if they start to thin or retreat from these anchoring points into deeper water behind, then they can retreat drastically through accelerated calving until they reach another stable position farther back. Their spectacular changes frequently attract media attention. For example, the Columbia Glacier in south central Alaska, which descends to Prince William Sound from the Chugach Mountains, has receded by over 7½ miles (12 kilometers) since 1984 and the rate is increasing. If this continues, a new fjord will be formed, similar to Glacier Bay. This contrasts with the behavior of the Hubbard Glacier, 249 miles (400 kilometers) to the southeast. It is the largest tidewater glacier in North America and has been called the 'galloping glacier'. It descends from the St Elias Mountains and terminates in a calving front in Disenchantment Bay. It has a history of repeated advances and retreats during the last thousand years. In spring 1986, it began a rapid advance that blocked off Russell Fjord, creating a lake in which the water level rose by over 80 feet (25 meters) and trapping many marine mammals and nesting birds. Overspill from the lake threatened to damage important salmon spawning grounds on the Situk River, near Yakutat. However, the ice dam burst after a few months, lowering the water level and removing the immediate threat.

The variable behavior of calving glaciers is also well illustrated by examples from Patagonia. Here, the glaciers were mostly retreating during the twentieth century. However, some tidewater and calving glaciers show very variable behavior. Glaciar Pío XI (tidewater) advanced by nearly 6 miles (10 kilometers) between 1945 and 1994. In contrast, Glaciar O'Higgins (lake calving) retreated 7 miles (11 kilometers) over the same period, while Glaciar Perito Moreno (also lake calving) has been relatively stable.

It is important to bear in mind such variability when using glaciers as indicators of climate change or when ascribing the behavior of individual glaciers, or spectacular events, to climate change. In particular, calving glaciers and surge-type glaciers are not good yardsticks.

Glaciar Perito Moreno, extends out from the South Patagonian icefield, terminating in a calving icefront.

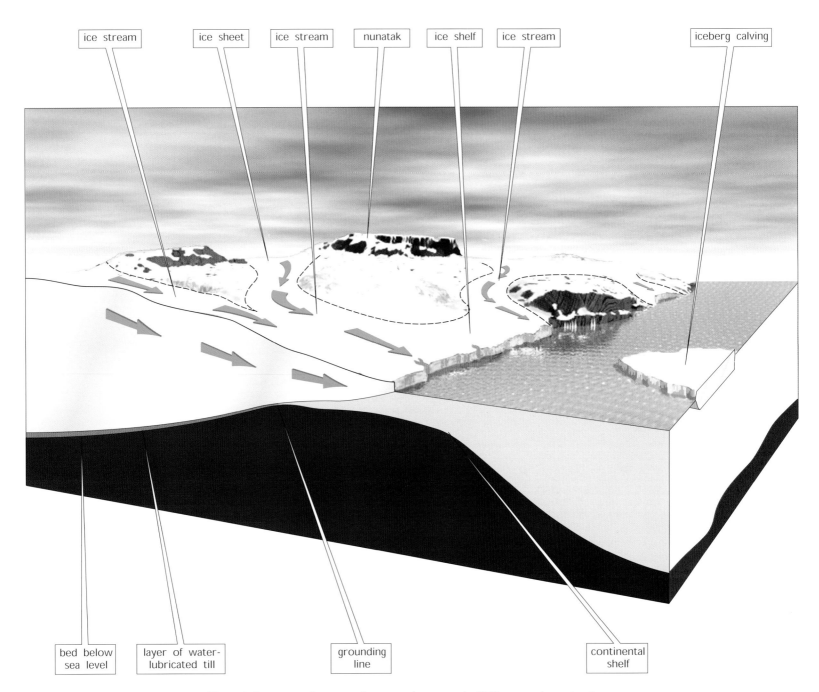

ice stream   ice sheet   ice stream   nunatak   ice shelf   ice stream   iceberg calving

bed below sea level   layer of water-lubricated till   grounding line   continental shelf

Typical features of an ice sheet and an ice shelf. The ice sheet is shown
with its bed below sea level, which is the case for the West Antarctic ice sheet.

Ice Sheets

The White Giants

Most of the world's glacier ice today is held in the vast Antarctic and Greenland ice sheets. Antarctica alone contains over 90 percent of the global ice volume. This represents about 70 percent of the world's freshwater, which if it melted, would raise sea level by about 213 feet (65 meters) – fortunately an unlikely prospect. The East Antarctic ice sheet covers an area greater than the United States and is over 13,000 feet (4000 meters) thick. The smaller West Antarctic ice sheet is grounded below sea level, up to 1½ miles (2½ kilometers) below in places, and covers an area approximately the size of Mexico. These huge ice sheets completely bury the landscape. Whole mountain ranges lie beneath the Antarctic ice, although sometimes their summits appear above the ice surface as 'nunataks'. Even more astonishingly, there are large lakes beneath the Antarctic ice sheet that have not seen the light of day for a million years or more. The ice sheets, particularly in Antarctica, play an important role in global climate processes. Also, buried in their layers, they contain remarkable archives of past climate change that tell a chilling tale of the ice age, of rapid switches in the climate and the advance and retreat of glaciers.

Ice sheets are large, dome-shaped bodies of ice. Typically, they have a relatively steep edge, but much more gentle upper slopes. This would have been evident to the parties of early Antarctic explorers – led by Scott, Shackleton and Amundsen – as they toiled to reach the polar plateau of the Antarctic ice sheet on which the South Pole is located. Ice sheets comprise areas of relatively slow-moving ice, flowing at only a few meters a year, and 'streams' of ice moving much faster. Hundreds of miles long and 30 miles (50 kilometers) wide, these ice streams are the powerhouses of the ice sheets. Like the great rivers that drain the continents, they are solid 'rivers' of ice that drain the ice sheets. They maintain the balance of the ice sheets, transferring ice from where it accumulates through snowfall to where it melts or is discharged into the sea through calving ice tongues or through ice shelves. Typically, ice streams flow at speeds of up to a mile or so per year. The fastest known ice stream, Jakobshavn Isbrae in West Greenland, flows at up to 4.4 miles (7 kilometers) per year near to its terminus. Such fast-moving ice streams are believed to be sliding on a layer of wet sediment.

Environmental Archives

The ice sheets are a particularly valuable source of information about past climates and environmental changes. Snow and ice accumulate in annual layers over the centuries and millennia, rather like the rings of a tree. By drilling down through the ice sheets, scientists are able to travel back in time and reconstruct the climate from the changing chemical composition of the ice, which acts as a natural thermometer. Also, as the snow and ice accumulate, tiny air bubbles are trapped and buried. These contain traces of the gases in the atmosphere at the time the bubbles were sealed in the ice, preserving a record of how the composition of the atmosphere has changed. Cores have now been drilled to depths of over 1.9 miles (3 kilometers) in the Greenland and Antarctic ice sheets and continuous samples of the ice recovered. The longest core, from Vostok Station in Antarctica, has provided a record of climate change over the last 420,000 years. Studies of these cores have revealed dramatic and regular fluctuations in climate. These fluctuations are also seen in the climate records from cores drilled in the sediments on the floors of the world's oceans. They reflect variations in the amount of solar radiation reaching the Earth due to variations in the Earth's orbit around the Sun. The records show a succession of intensely cold periods ('glacials') lasting up to 100,000 years, punctuated by warmer periods ('interglacials') with climates like that of the present and lasting about 10,000 years. On a geological timescale, we are living today in the latter half of an interglacial, which began about 10,000 years ago. The natural tendency is for the climate to get colder as we start to enter the next glacial period.

The ice cores have also allowed insights into more recent climate changes. Acidic layers (from the deposition of sulphuric acid) in ice cores from Greenland record the history of volcanic eruptions, including that of Tambora in the East Indies in 1815, which was followed by the 'year without a summer' when crops failed in New England due to

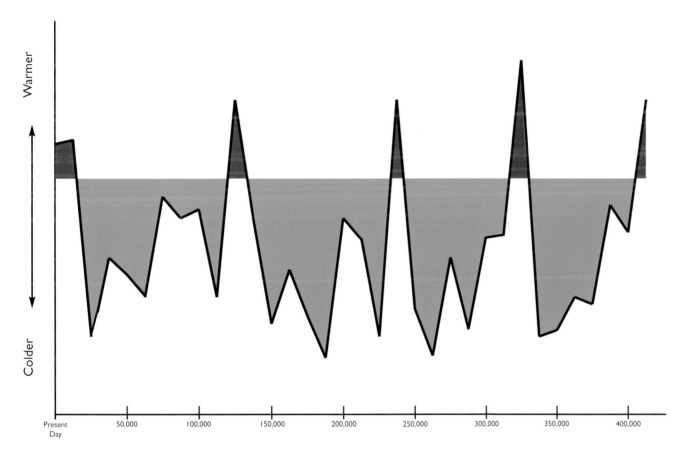

The climate records obtained from Antarctic ice sheet cores show repeated and rapid fluctuations between warm and cold conditions over the last 420,000 years. The warm peaks (interglacials), like that of today, are relatively short-lived.

disastrous summer frosts. Earlier, the Greenland ice core records show a series of cold spells that contributed in part to the failure of the Norse settlements in Greenland in the fourteenth and fifteenth centuries. At the time of the original settlers' arrival at the end of the tenth century, the climate was relatively more hospitable.

In relation to global warming, the ice cores have provided a picture of the changes in carbon dioxide in the atmosphere over time and allowed a comparison of present-day levels of this 'greenhouse' gas with the natural background levels. These comparisons show that present levels are now higher than at any time in the last 420,000 years.

Rising levels of atmospheric pollution since the Industrial Revolution are also apparent in the ice cores. Contaminants such as heavy metals and organic compounds (DDT and PCBs) have been measured in the surface layers of the Greenland and Antarctic ice sheets. Concentrations of lead in snow deposited in Greenland in the 1960s show levels 200 times higher than in the past, reflecting the use of lead additives in petrol. However, values have decreased since 1970 following restrictions on their use in the U.S.A. and Europe. Cores from Greenland have revealed even earlier episodes of atmospheric pollution from the mining and smelting of lead, silver and copper during the Greek and Roman periods some 2000 years ago. The period of nuclear weapons testing in the atmosphere before the Partial Test Ban Treaty in 1963, is also recorded in the radioactive fallout from nuclear bomb tests preserved in the surface layers of the ice, as is the fallout from the accident at Chernobyl in 1986. Ironically, such 'radioactive' layers provide useful time-markers for scientists studying the ice core records.

In Antarctica, local patterns of glacier flow have provided unusually rich sources of meteorites. These have fallen onto the ice and been buried by the accumulation of snow and ice over thousands of years. However, in some areas where the ice is melting, known as 'blue ice' areas, the upward flow of the glacier has brought them back to the bare surface of the ice where they form concentrations. These blue ice areas are an important source of materials for the study of extraterrestrial rocks. One of the most famous

Melting has etched out structures in the bare ice surface of Dyngjujökull, Vatnajökull ice cap, Iceland.

meteorite finds included tube-like structures that generated much debate about the possible existence of life on Mars.

Lakes Beneath the Ice

As outlined above, water can exist in a thin layer at the bottom of a glacier under certain conditions where the ice is very thick or fast moving. However, one remarkable phenomenon is the occurrence of some 70 large lakes underneath the Antarctic ice sheet.

Crevassed surface of Campbell Glacier, Antarctica.

The largest, Lake Vostok, is about the size of Lake Ontario and in places may be as much as 1640-3280 feet (500-1000 meters) deep. It is located under the Russian scientific station, Vostok, in one of the least accessible and coldest parts of Antarctica. Its presence was first revealed in the 1970s when the ice sheet was surveyed using ice-penetrating radar. Subsequently, it was confirmed on satellite images by a large flat area on the surface of the ice. The lake has been isolated from the rest of the world beneath some 2½ miles (4 kilometers) of ice, possibly for more than a million years, and may contain unique microorganisms that have evolved under the most extreme living conditions on the planet. Understandably, scientists are keen to obtain samples from the lake, but in doing so, there is a very high risk of contaminating the water. In fact, a team of glaciologists had already been drilling down through the ice in the area to obtain ice cores for studies of the Earth's climate history. This coring ceased about 325 feet (100 meters) above the lake to prevent the drill breaking through and contaminating the unique environment with drilling fluid. Proposals have been discussed for sending a sterilized robotic probe down through a drill hole in the ice and into the lake with instruments to look for life and recover samples. However, environmentalists have questioned whether this can be done without introducing contamination into the lake. From a wider viewpoint,

Outlet glaciers descend steeply from the Vatnajökull ice cap to the coast, southeast Iceland.

exploration of Lake Vostok could provide an ideal opportunity for NASA scientists to test the technology for probing the ice of Europa, one of Jupiter's moons believed to be a potential source of extraterrestrial life in a similar environment to Lake Vostok.

Ice Sheets – Stable or Unstable?

The stability of the polar ice sheets has attracted considerable scientific as well as media attention because of the catastrophic effects their rapid melting or collapse would have on global sea level. A rising sea level would lead to the drowning of lower-lying coasts, such as those of the Mississippi, large parts of Florida, the Nile delta and Bangladesh, and the disappearance of islands in the Pacific Ocean.

One particular concern has centered on the stability of the West Antarctic ice sheet and its ice streams which, if they collapsed, could raise the world sea level by about 16½ feet (5 meters). What distinguishes this ice sheet is that much of its bed lies below present sea level, so that it might be vulnerable to the kind of rapid recession seen in some calving icefronts such as the Columbia Glacier, but on a much greater scale. Also, because the ice streams are fast moving, they could potentially draw down the ice sheet very quickly.

The West Antarctic ice sheet first formed several millions of years ago, but whether or not it has melted and reformed since then is unclear. The discovery of the remains of microscopic marine plants in cores taken from the bottom of the ice sheet suggests that this may have happened in the past. Also, there is evidence that sea levels were higher than at present during one or more past interglacials, implying a significant reduction in the volume of polar ice. However, glaciologists now believe that the West Antarctic ice sheet is unlikely to collapse in the next few hundred years and that its future behavior is likely to be rather more complex. Both the East Antarctic and Greenland ice sheets contain greater volumes of ice, equivalent to a sea level rise of 171 feet (52 meters) and 23 feet (7 meters), respectively. However, in contrast to the West Antarctic ice sheet, they are land-based and, therefore, not vulnerable to rapid collapse through accelerated calving.

Mountain ranges lie buried beneath the Antarctic ice sheet, with the summits appearing as nunataks.

Ice Shelves

Floating Ice and Giant Icebergs

Ice shelves are thick floating masses of ice. They form through the extension of glaciers from the land into the sea and by snow accumulation on their surface. They may be 650 feet (200 meters) thick at their seaward edge and deform under their own weight. The area where the ice starts to float is known as the 'grounding line'. The largest ice shelves in the world are in Antarctica, in the Ross Sea (Ross Ice Shelf) and the Weddell Sea (Filchner and Ronne Ice Shelves). The Ross Ice Shelf covers an area the size of Texas and the combined Filchner-Ronne Ice Shelf is slightly smaller. Many smaller ice shelves occur along the Antarctic Peninsula and there are several in the Canadian Arctic. Along their outer margins, ice shelves form largely unbroken ice cliffs rising up to 100 feet (30 meters) above the level of the sea. Thus, when early

As they drift in the ocean, icebergs weather into unusual shapes.

Antarctic explorers encountered the Ross Ice Shelf, named after its discoverer James Clark Ross, they christened it the 'Great Barrier' since it provided few weaknesses that might allow a landfall.

Ice shelves play an important part in the glacier balance of Antarctica. Much of the continental ice of Antarctica flows into ice shelves where it is lost by calving of icebergs into the sea. Periodically, huge tabular masses of ice break off and float out into the

The glacial world of the Neumayer Channel, Antarctic Peninsula.

Southern Ocean. This is part of a natural and ongoing process. One of largest icebergs ever sighted, in 1956 from the *USS Glacier*, was over 200 miles (320 kilometers) long and 60 miles (96 kilometers) wide and probably came from the Ross Ice Shelf.

Today, thanks to the availability of satellite images, it is possible to monitor iceberg calving events from afar. For example, in October 1998, a large iceberg calved from the Ronne Ice Shelf. It was 90 miles (145 kilometers) long and 31 miles (50 kilometers) wide (about one-and-a-half times the area of Delaware). Three further large icebergs followed in May 2000. The loss of these icebergs has returned the edge of the ice shelf back to the position where it was in the 1950s. Thus over time, there is a tendency for ice shelves to maintain a stable position.

In March 2000, an even bigger iceberg detached from the Ross Ice Shelf. With a size of 183 miles (295 kilometers) long by 23 miles (37 kilometers) wide, it was nearly as large as Connecticut. It calved from near the Bay of Whales, a natural embayment that forms a permanent feature in the front edge of the shelf, where the ice flows around Roosevelt Island. This bay was the site of 'Framheim', the base used by the Norwegian explorer, Roald Admunsen, for his journey to the South Pole in 1911. Later, Admiral Richard E Byrd used the same area for a series of bases, called 'Little America', from which he carried out extensive aerial surveys. His achievements also included the first flight over the South Pole in 1929. These bases were subsequently all carried out to sea on the surface of icebergs, which broke away from the ice shelf. Such calving events are not unusual and there is no evidence that they represent a response to climate warming. The edge of the Ross Ice Shelf is currently in places further north than its average position in the last 150 years.

Antarctic icebergs are a potential hazard to shipping in the Southern Ocean – mainly research vessels, re-supply ships for the scientific stations, cruise ships and fishing vessels – but the level of traffic is generally low and the bergs can be tracked by satellite as they drift along the coast and eventually northwards. As they move northwards, the large tabular bergs break up into smaller bergs and take on more fantastic shapes.

The large volume of ice lost from Antarctica each year through the calving of icebergs represents a potentially valuable source of freshwater. It has been suggested that

Small floating ice shelf bordering the Dugdale and Murray Glaciers, Admiralty Mountains, Victoria Land, Antarctica. A tabular iceberg has recently calved from the front of the ice shelf.

The spectacular Lemaire Channel is one of the highlights
on tourist ship itineraries to the Antarctic Peninsula.

large icebergs could be towed to arid parts of the Southern Hemisphere, such as the Atacama Desert in Chile, Western Australia and the Namib Desert of southern Africa. All these areas have cold surface currents offshore, which would help to reduce melting en route and towing costs. As well as providing a water supply, the melted water could be utilized in the generation of electricity through a thermal energy conversion process. However, there are many practical and economic uncertainties and the ideas remain on the drawing board.

Ice Today – Gone Tomorrow

The loss of large icebergs by calving is a normal process that is generally balanced by surface accumulation and inputs of ice from landward glaciers. However, dramatic changes of a different nature have recently affected a number of the more northern ice shelves on the Antarctic Peninsula. Although these ice shelves have been retreating for the last 50 years, the recent changes are exceptional,

Remnant of a tabular iceberg.

leading to the complete break up and disappearance of certain ice shelves. On the west side of the Peninsula, the Wordie Ice Shelf effectively collapsed between 1966 and the end of the 1980s. On the east side, the northern Larsen Ice Shelf disintegrated completely in 1995, a process that is graphically displayed on satellite images taken at the time. A large part of this break up took place within a few days, sending thousands of small icebergs into the Weddell Sea.

At the same time, part of the shelf that formerly connected James Ross Island to the Antarctic Peninsula also disappeared completely, so that the island is now circumnavigable during the Antarctic summer for the first time in recorded history. Farther south on the Peninsula, the Larsen B and Wilkins Ice Shelves are now showing signs of accelerated retreat.

The disintegration of these ice shelves generated considerable attention in the media and was portrayed by environmental groups as a direct effect, and, hence, early warning, of global warming. Temperature records from meteorological stations on the Peninsula do show an overall rise in temperatures of 4.5°F (2.5°C) in the area over the last 50 years. Therefore, the loss of the ice shelves may be seen as an effect of this regional warming. However, it is too early to say whether it is other than a natural fluctuation or to ascribe it to global warming. The effects are confined to a small part of the Antarctic, and there is no evidence that similar changes are imminent elsewhere.

Ice cliff, South Shetland Islands, Antarctica.

In climatic terms, the ice shelves on the Antarctic Peninsula are at the northern limit of viability and, hence, are the most sensitive to climate changes. It is likely that they have experienced previous cycles of growth and decay, reflecting climate changes in the past. There is a strong possibility that at least some of them disappeared during the warmer climatic conditions that occurred about 5000 years ago, and they then re-formed at some time within the last few thousand years.

The loss of the ice shelves on the Antarctic Peninsula will not contribute to a rise in sea level because they were already floating and displacing an equivalent volume of sea water. Also, their disappearance will not affect the stability of the West Antarctic ice sheet and is unlikely to destabilize adjacent land-based glaciers.

Calving icefront, Paradise Bay, Antarctic Peninsula.

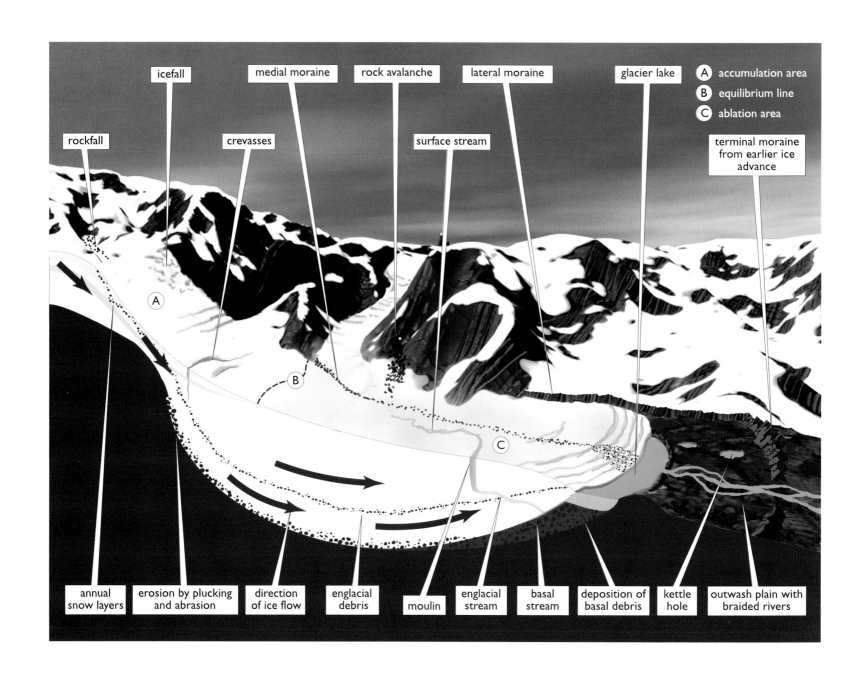

icefall medial moraine rock avalanche lateral moraine glacier lake

(A) accumulation area
(B) equilibrium line
(C) ablation area

rockfall crevasses surface stream

terminal moraine from earlier ice advance

annual snow layers erosion by plucking and abrasion direction of ice flow englacial debris moulin englacial stream basal stream deposition of basal debris kettle hole outwash plain with braided rivers

Typical features of a mountain glacier and its associated landforms.

Mountain Glaciers

Alpine World

Several types of glacier exist in mountain areas. Ice caps are dome-shaped bodies of ice, smaller than ice sheets. A good example is Vatnajökull in Iceland. Icefields are flat or sloping areas of ice that lack the dome shape of ice caps, and their surface is frequently interrupted by mountain ridges and summits. The St Elias Mountains icefield is the largest area of ice in North America, and the North and South Patagonian icefields in the southern Andes are the largest glaciers outside the polar areas.

Many smaller ice caps and icefields occur in Norway and the Canadian Arctic. Both ice caps and icefields have faster moving areas of ice, known as 'outlet glaciers', which drain their interiors. Like the ice streams in the ice sheets, outlet glaciers are usually lubricated by water or wet sediments at their beds, and are powerful agents of erosion. Where they enter the sea, for example along the fjord coast of south central and southeast Alaska, they are described as 'tidewater' glaciers.

'Corrie' or 'cirque' glaciers are small glaciers located in valley heads or semi-circular mountain basins. Often they extend down-valley as valley glaciers. Corrie and valley glaciers are common in mountain areas.

Mountain glaciers are responsible for many of the spectacular glacial landforms in classic 'alpine' landscapes such as the Alps, Himalayas, Southern Alps of New Zealand and the ranges of western North America. As they flow, valley glaciers deepen their beds, quarrying and abrading the bedrock. The resulting landforms include rock steps and basins in the valley bottoms, the former often filled by lakes when the ice melts back. The rocks display polished and striated surfaces, and often have distinctive 'whaleback' forms. Sometimes these are broken on their down-valley sides where the rock has been quarried by the ice. Such characteristic glacial forms are known as 'roches moutonnées' because they were thought to resemble eighteenth-century wigs, known as 'moutonnées', which were held in shape with mutton fat. A large example is Lembert Dome in Tuolumne Meadows, in Yosemite National Park.

The debris from erosion of the glacier bed is transported underneath the ice and in the basal layers of the ice. However, the bed is not the only source of supply of rock debris to alpine glaciers. Rockfalls from adjacent mountain cliffs frequently add material to the surface of the ice. Some of this is buried by snow and is carried along within the glaciers. Often it is transported on the glacier surface as very distinctive stripes of rock debris, known as 'medial moraines'. On some glaciers, the debris melts out to form an extensive cover over the ice surface in the ablation area, insulating the ice and retarding its melting. Occasionally, large rock avalanches can add massive amounts of debris onto the surface of a glacier. A notable example happened in Alaska on the Sherman Glacier, in the Chugach Mountains, following the 1964 earthquake. A more recent instance occurred in New Zealand in 1991 on the Tasman Glacier below Mount Cook.

Glaciers, therefore, act as giant conveyor belts, transporting rock debris at their beds, on their surfaces and within their internal layers. This material is then deposited in a variety of forms, comprising a mixture of stones, boulders, clay and silt, known as 'till'. 'Lateral moraines' form along the glacier margins. 'End moraines' occur where the debris piles up at the glacier fronts. Where glaciers are advancing, large ridges may be pushed up. Where they are melting back, a succession of 'recessional moraines' may be formed. Geologists are often able to date these moraines and to reconstruct the past history of glacier changes and, hence, infer past changes in climate.

Water is a characteristic feature of most mountain glacier margins in summer. Meltwater rivers emerge from tunnels beneath the ice, and frequently shift their courses across the unstable sand and gravel deposits of their outwash plains. The rate of ice melting varies during the day according to the air temperature, so that water levels in glacial rivers also fluctuate, but with a time lag. They are usually at their lowest in the early morning and highest later in the day, an important consideration when hiking in glaciated mountains where there are no footbridges.

Medial moraines on the Malaspina Glacier, Alaska, the largest piedmont glacier in the world.

Glaciers Come and Go

Mountain glaciers are constantly adjusting to the natural rhythm of climate change and have been doing so throughout the ice age. In historical times, most mountain glaciers reached more advanced positions, although not always at the same time, during the 'Little Ice Age' of the sixteenth to the nineteenth centuries. These advances have been documented in contemporary writing, paintings and early photographs, particularly in the Alps, Norway and Iceland. The positions reached by the glaciers are usually marked by prominent terminal and lateral moraine ridges. Following glacier recession since the mid-nineteenth century, the Little Ice Age terminal moraines now generally occur some distance down-valley from the present glacier fronts, and lateral moraines rise steeply above the lowered glacier surfaces.

The recent recession of mountain glaciers has produced some interesting surprises. In parts of the Alps and Alaska, for example, the retreating glaciers have revealed the remains of trees and vegetation underneath the ice. Radiocarbon dating of these materials shows them to be several thousands of years old, indicating that the glaciers have been less extensive in the past and that forests grew farther up the valleys. Astonishingly, in 1991, in the Tyrolean Alps, the corpse of a 5000-year-old Neolithic man was discovered. Named 'Oetzi', he appears to have been in his mid-forties and perished while crossing a high pass on the border between Italy and Austria. His body had lain frozen and preserved in the ice and snow all that time until re-exposed by the recent melting. It has even been possible to identify his last meal from the contents of his stomach. It included mountain goat and wheat products. Medically, he suffered from arthrosis, hardening of the arteries, chilblains and intestinal worms. Marks on his body even suggest that he had undergone a form of acupuncture. In a similar find in 1999, the well-preserved remains of a 600-year-old Indian hunter emerged from a melting glacier in British Columbia, together with bows, arrows and spears. Such remains provide unique insights into nutrition, health and how people lived in the past. Other

Crevasse patterns, Skálafellsjökull, Iceland.

recent revelations have included aircraft that had crashed on glaciers and disappeared in Iceland and the Andes during and shortly after World War Two.

Mountain Glacier Hazards

In many parts of the world, glacier recession since the mid-nineteenth century has allowed the formation of lakes behind the Little Ice Age terminal moraines. The moraine dams, which hold up these lakes, are often unstable and liable to fail, resulting in sudden outburst floods from the lakes. Such lakes are common in the Cordillera of western Canada and several are known to have drained suddenly in this way. Fortunately, these occurrences have been in remote areas. Elsewhere, however, such floods have posed a real threat to human life and infrastructure, particularly in the Himalayas and the Andes. Where large rock and ice avalanches have fallen into the lakes from adjacent mountains, the resulting waves have overtopped and breached the moraine dams. One such event occurred at Dig Tsho in the Khumbu region of Nepal in 1985, when the resulting flood on the Dudh Kosi destroyed a nearly completed power plant at Namche Bazaar, 7½ miles (12 kilometers) downstream. Houses, trails, bridges and valuable agricultural land were also destroyed. Should a similar outburst occur from the nearby lake at Imja Glacier, it could have devastating consequences on settlements downstream and the trekking industry, which is crucial to the economy of this area.

In the Cordillera Blanca of Peru, there have been many devastating glacial lake outbursts in the last few hundred years. One of the most disastrous occurred in 1941, when a flood of mud, boulders and ice destroyed one third of the city of Huaraz and killed more than 6000 people. Since then, measures have been taken to lower lake levels by excavating channels or diversion tunnels through the moraine dams. Such precautions, however, cannot prevent the catastrophic effects of major ice and rock avalanches. Again in the Cordillera Blanca, a huge flow of ice, mud and rock was initiated by an ice avalanche from Huascarán Norte in 1962. This accelerated down-valley and engulfed the town of Yungay, some 10 miles (16 kilometers) away, in about eight minutes. The death toll was 4000. In 1982, an even greater catastrophe occurred. Part of the same mountain

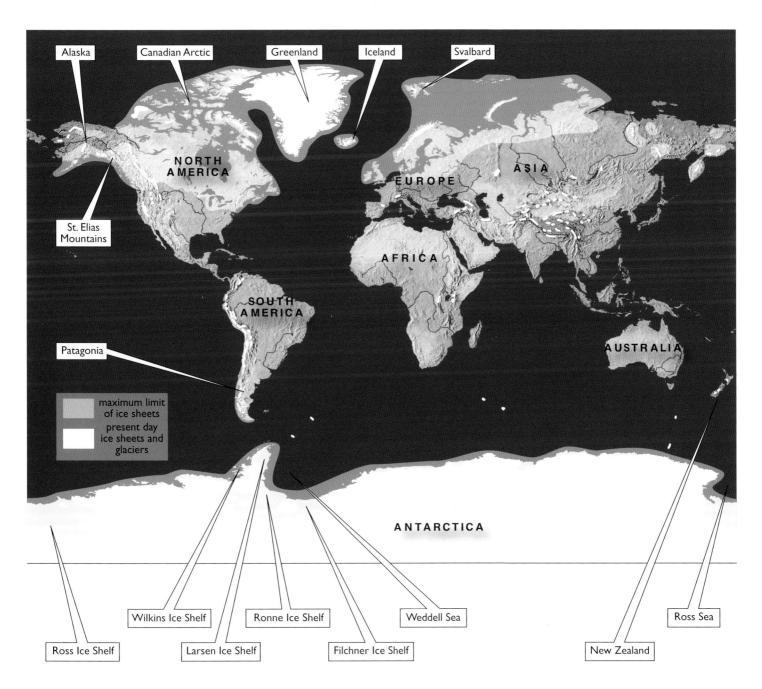

World distribution of glaciers today and the maximum extent of former ice sheets.
(Sea ice extent and former ice shelves are not shown.)

collapsed during an earthquake and the resulting landslide, lubricated by melted ice, again devastated Yungay. The town was buried in mud, rock and ice and an estimated 18,000 people were killed. In the European Alps, an ice avalanche from the Allalin Glacier killed 88 construction workers at the site of the Mattmark Dam in 1965.

Glacial lake outburst floods also occur where lakes dammed along the margins of glaciers drain suddenly when the ice dam fails. Several examples occur regularly in Alaska and the western Cordillera of Canada, fortunately in areas where the threats to human activities are low.

A combination of glaciers and volcanoes presents a particularly high-level of hazard. The eruption of a volcano under a glacier can generate huge amounts of melting and large floods that drain from the front of the glacier. High levels of heat also favor the formation of subglacial lakes. These are released periodically as vast floods, known as 'jökulhlaups' (glacier bursts) in Iceland. Here, every ten years or so, the high geothermal heat from a volcano under the Vatnajökull ice cap builds up the level of Grímsvötn, until the ice dam fails. The water from the lake drains underneath the ice cap and bursts out from the front of the glacier some 30 miles (50 kilometers) away. The massive floods may last for two to three weeks and are particularly damaging to infrastructure. The last flood, following a volcanic eruption in 1996, swept away the main coastal road in south Iceland and caused damage to bridges, electric lines and telephone cables estimated at 10-15 million US dollars. Where glaciers melt rapidly during volcanic eruptions, fast-moving mudflows or 'lahars' are a high risk to life and property. During the 1985 eruption of the Nevada del Ruiz volcano in Columbia, such mudflows swept down the mountainside, destroying several villages in their paths and resulting in the deaths of 23,000 people.

Where glaciers enter the sea, the calving of icebergs represents a potential hazard to shipping, often far from the glacier source. Ocean currents regularly carry flotillas of icebergs from Greenland to the Grand Banks off Newfoundland. Here in 1912, the SS *Titanic* had its famous and disastrous collision with such an iceberg. A more recent

Glaciers cover the summit and upper slopes of Mount Rainier, a dormant volcano in Washington, U.S.A.

instance where icebergs have been implicated in a shipping accident occurred in Alaska in 1989, when the oil tanker, *Exxon Valdez*, ran aground. The tanker is believed to have changed course to avoid ice in western Valdez Arm of Prince William Sound, which had calved from the front of Columbia Glacier.

Mountain Glaciers and Water Resources

Glaciers store water in the form of snow and ice during winter and release it in summer. Therefore, in many of the drier parts of the world, they are an important source of water supply for public consumption, irrigation and hydroelectric power generation. Large cities such as La Paz and Lima obtain their water from glaciers, and major rivers such as the Indus and Ganges have glacier sources. It was even recently reported in the press that the authorities in Pakistan were considering the spreading of charcoal onto glacier surfaces to increase their rate of melting to help alleviate the effects of a drought in the northern part of the country.

In the Alps and Norway, glaciers are an important source of water for hydroelectric power. In Norway, the water is collected in systems of tunnels drilled in the bedrock underneath the glaciers. In the Alps, large dams have been built to store the water. In parts of the Himalayas and the Andes, waterpower from glacier sources has a significant part to play in economic development in mountain communities.

Mountain Glaciers – a Tourist Attraction

Historically, glaciers and the spectacular scenery of glaciated landscapes have been a well-established tourist attraction in areas like the Alps and Norway. They now form major attractions in many other parts of the world, and feature in cruise itineraries to Alaska, Chile and the Antarctic. The spectacular calving glaciers of Glacier Bay National Park in Alaska attract a quarter of a million visitors a year. The regular calving of ice from their fronts provides an exciting spectacle for visitors on cruise ships and private boats. Visitors can obtain even closer contact with the ice at Athabasca Glacier in Canada, where tours on tracked vehicles go up onto the glacier.

Glacier tour on snowmobiles, Vatnajökull, Iceland.

Ice Age Ancestors

An Icy Planet

The Earth's climate record shows that ice ages have occurred many times in the past and that glaciers have advanced and retreated over timescales from decades to millions of years. At its most extreme, between 800 and 600 million years ago, ice may have covered the entire globe, forming what has graphically been described as a 'snowball Earth'.

The present ice age began about two-and-a-half million years ago. During this time, vast ice sheets have expanded several times across the middle latitudes of Europe and North America and have dramatically shaped the landscape. The present ice age, however, has not been one long episode of a 'snowball Earth'. The climate records from the ice cores and ocean floor sediments reveal that there have been many long, cold episodes (glacials), broken by shorter, warmer intervals (interglacials). Today we live in one of the interglacials. However, the records show that such periods are relatively short-lived on a geological timescale. The world today would be very different if civilization had developed during a glacial period when large areas of North America and Europe were covered by ice sheets.

During the coldest parts of the present ice age, the northern ice sheets moved south. At its maximum extent, the North American, or Laurentide, ice sheet covered most of Canada and the central and northeast United States. The southern limit of the ice ran from central Montana, through the Dakotas, Nebraska and eastern Kansas, south of the Great Lakes through Missouri and Kentucky, and northeast to New England, where it lay offshore. The maximum thickness of the ice may have reached 1½ miles (2½ kilometers). In the west, the Laurentide ice sheet merged with a separate ice sheet that covered the Cordillera from Puget Sound to the Yukon and parts of Alaska. In the northeast, it merged with the Innuitian ice sheet over the Canadian Arctic islands.

In Europe, ice expanded out from centers in the Scandinavian mountains. It moved

Mount McKinley towers above the snow-covered Ruth Glacier, Denali National Park, Alaska.

north over the Barents Sea, east into northern Siberia and south into central Europe, Poland and Germany. At its maximum extent, this ice sheet merged across the North Sea with a smaller ice sheet in Britain, which extended almost as far south as London.

Mountain areas like the Alps, Andes, Himalayas and Rockies had expanded icefields, and the ice sheets in Greenland and Antarctica were larger than today.

Areas immediately beyond the ice sheets experienced intensely cold, tundra climates. Frozen ground ('permafrost') was widespread and extensive areas of windblown dust, known as 'loess', accumulated in the dry interior parts of the continents in the mid-west of the United States, central and eastern Europe and China, where the fine-grained sediments were winnowed out by the wind from sparsely vegetated ground.

The last ice sheets generally reached their maximum extents about 22,000 years ago. Rapid climate warming after about 15,000 years ago saw significant shrinkage, although final disappearance of the North American and European ice sheets did not occur until some time after the further sustained warming around 11,500 years ago that ushered in the present interglacial.

Landscape Legacy

The glaciers deepened the pre-existing river valleys and sometimes even created new valleys where none existed before. They carved out the glens of Scotland with their famous lochs, such as Loch Ness, and the valleys of the Finger Lakes in New York State. Such glacial valleys or 'troughs' have a distinctive shape. They are often described as 'U-shaped', which is correct in parts of the Alps, Yosemite and the Southern Alps of New Zealand. Most, however, have less steep sides and a more parabolic form when seen in profile. Where main valleys were deepened more than their tributaries, the latter were left hanging, so that their junctions now often form the sites of spectacular waterfalls. Bridal Veil falls in Yosemite is a good example. At the coast, where glacial troughs have been drowned by the sea, the resulting fjords now form a wonderful scenic attraction.

Glaciers eroded the Great Glen in Scotland along the line of an ancient fault in the bedrock.

Although Norway is renowned for its fjords, they are also a feature of the glaciated coasts of southeast Alaska, New Zealand and Chile. In all these areas, the glaciated landscape provides the basis for important tourist industries, involving ship cruises amid the stunning scenery.

Another landform particularly characteristic of glaciated mountains is the 'corrie' or 'cirque'. These mountain basins, often the home to small glaciers today, have a steep headwall and a flatter floor often scoured out by glacial erosion and now occupied by a

Boulder abandoned by a former glacier, Yosemite.

small lake. Such corries have a wonderful atmosphere of the high mountains, and their rock walls provide challenges for rock and ice climbing. Corries often develop in clusters, so that when viewed from the air, it appears as if a giant biscuit cutter has been used to take scallops out of the mountain. Over time, erosion may reduce the dividing areas between adjacent corries to narrow ridges or 'arêtes'. Sometimes, these may be lowered, leaving an isolated mountain pyramid, or 'horn', such as the Matterhorn in the Alps or Mount Aspiring in New Zealand.

In lowland areas, where the ice sheets were sliding on rocky beds, they scoured the landscape extensively, forming ice-scraped hills and lake-filled depressions that follow lines of geological weakness. Such landscapes are typical of the Canadian Shield, West Greenland and western Norway. The ice also excavated the deep basins now occupied by the Great Lakes, Lake Winnipeg, Great Bear Lake and Great Slave Lake.

At a smaller scale, ice-molded or 'streamlined' hills are typical of many lowland glaciated areas. In central Scotland, the resistant cores of ancient volcanoes have locally protected weaker sedimentary rocks on their lee sides, forming what are known as 'crag and tail' landforms. A classic example occurs in the center of Edinburgh – Scotland's capital city – where the rock on which the famous castle is built forms the crag and the street known as the Royal Mile occupies the tail. This shows how

Glaciated mountain scenery, Heavy Runner Mountain, Glacier National Park, Montana.

glacial landforms are even a feature of our urban landscapes.

In some mountain areas, the effects of ice erosion were selective. In parts of Labrador, Baffin Island and the Cairngorm Mountains in Scotland, the glaciers excavated deep valleys through the mountains, but left intervening plateau surfaces relatively unmodified. This reflects a contrast between the presence of fast, sliding ice streams and outlet glaciers in the valleys and rather slow-moving ice frozen to the bedrock elsewhere.

The ice sheets covered large areas of Europe and North America in a blanket of till, which now forms the parent materials for many of our agricultural soils. This till was deposited underneath the ice and was often shaped and molded by the ice into a variety of streamlined landforms. One characteristic type is 'drumlins'. These oval-shaped hills often occur in groups, for example, in west central New York, Wisconsin and Ontario. More elongated forms, known as 'flutes', formed in North Dakota, Montana and Saskatchewan.

South and west of the Great Lakes, extensive systems of moraines identify former ice margin positions. Northwest into Minnesota, the Dakotas, Saskatchewan and Alberta, deposition occurred on the surface of the ice, resulting in the formation of extensive belts of morainic hills many miles wide when the underlying ice melted.

'Erratic' boulders differ from the local bedrock where they were dropped by the ice, sometimes hundreds of miles from their sources. They can be used to trace the former direction of ice flow. The dispersal of rocks in this way can be useful in mineral exploration to locate source areas of ore deposits.

During the retreat of the ice sheets, great rivers of meltwater were released. Traces of these long-gone rivers can now be seen in the landscape as dry channels formed along the margins or underneath the former glaciers. Often the ice controlled the flow of water, so that a distinctive characteristic of glacial channels is that they run along hillsides at a low angle and in positions that no modern river could occupy. Occasionally, they even run uphill where the water was forced against the gradient by the immense pressures under the ice. Former courses of glacial rivers are also sometimes delineated by sinuous ridges

A landscape shaped by glaciers – Lake Moraine, Banff National Park, Alberta.

of sand and gravel known as 'eskers'. These formed in ice-walled tunnels underneath the ice and were left stranded when the ice melted. In Canada, Sweden and Finland, eskers trace out the courses of former glacial rivers over tens of kilometers. Meltwater rivers also deposited large amounts of sand and gravel in the outwash plains in front of the ice sheets. Where these deposits were laid down on top of the glacier margin, the later melting of the buried ice produced a hummocky landscape of low hills and lake-filled depressions called 'kettle holes'.

Huge glacial lakes, now vanished, were ponded along the margins of the retreating North American ice sheet. The largest, Lake Agassiz, covered an area in Manitoba, Ontario, Saskatchewan, Minnesota and the Dakotas, greater than the present Great Lakes combined. Linked networks of spillways drained many of the lakes and now form dry, abandoned channels in the landscape. Some of the most remarkable landforms are associated with the catastrophic drainage of Glacial Lake Missoula in Montana. The volume of water in the lake was comparable to Lake Ontario and may have drained, probably on several occasions, in the space of a few days. The floodwaters swept 550 miles (880 kilometers) across an area of Washington and Idaho on their way to the Pacific Ocean down the Columbia valley. In doing so, they formed the so-called 'Channeled Scablands', now a vast area of huge flood channels, dry waterfalls and flat table-lands or 'scabs' between the channels, not unlike parts of the surface of Mars.

Sea-Level Changes

One indirect consequence of the growth and melting of the ice sheets was changes in land and sea levels. The great volume of water locked up in the ice sheets was sufficient to lower world sea level by some 390 feet (120 meters) during the major glaciations. The weight of ice on the continents also depressed the surface of the land. Thus there was a complex interplay between changing land and sea levels. Following the melting of the ice, the land recovered and sea level rose again.

Spring melt in the high arctic, Bylot Island, Canada.

Glaciers in the Future

Today we are still in the ice age, although, fortunately, in one of the warmer interglacials. The message from the geological record is that the climate is likely to start cooling in a few thousand years time, but that it may take about 50,000 years before large ice sheets spread once again over North America and Europe. A big uncertainty, however, concerns the role of global warming. Will it delay the process, as seems likely, or even reverse it? Or does the climate have some other surprises up its sleeve?

The climate record from the ice cores shows that changes can happen very quickly. There are also many complex links and feedbacks involving climate, the oceans, ice sheets and the biological life of the planet that are not fully understood. However, human activity has now so changed large parts of the planet that natural checks and balances may be disrupted. For example, if accelerated global warming produces rapid melting of Arctic sea ice and glaciers, this could provide a layer of freshwater on the surface of the North Atlantic Ocean and shut down the Gulf Stream that warms western Europe, throwing it into another Little Ice Age and possibly worse.

Mountain Glaciers

Global temperatures have increased by 1.1°F (0.6°C) since the middle of the nineteenth century. Most of this warming occurred in two phases, from about 1910 to 1945 and since the mid-1970s. This warming has been reflected in the deteriorating state of health of most mountain glaciers. In the Alps, the total area of glaciers has reduced by some 30-40 percent since the middle of the nineteenth century and many smaller glaciers may disappear in the next few decades. In the Canadian Rockies, the area covered by glaciers has decreased by about 25 percent over the same period. In Glacier National Park, Montana, the number of glaciers has declined from over 150 in 1850 to less than 50 today. The extent of the recession of the remaining glaciers can

Meltwater torrent at the front of Kjenndalsbreen, an outlet of the Jostedalsbreen ice cap, Norway.

be seen from comparisons of old and modern photographs, and even these glaciers could disappear in the next few decades. When George Vancouver explored the southeast coast of Alaska in 1794, the glaciers extended to the mouths of the fjords, and Glacier Bay was filled with ice where cruise ships sail today. John Muir Glacier, named after the famous explorer and conservationist, has now retreated some 31 miles (50 kilometers) from where he saw it in 1879.

Glaciers in the Himalayas have also receded considerably and one report has even predicted that all the glaciers in the central and eastern parts of the area could disappear by 2035 if the present rate of recession continues. Tropical glaciers have been particularly badly affected, notably since the 1980s. Lewis Glacier on Mount Kenya is now one third of its area in the 1920s, and the ice cover on Kilimanjaro declined by 82 percent between 1912 and 2000. In the Peruvian Andes, the retreat of the Quelccaya ice cap increased from 10 feet (3 meters) per year between the 1970s and 1990s to 100 feet (30 meters) per year in the 1990s.

In contrast, some glaciers in the maritime parts of Norway and Iceland have been advancing due to higher winter snowfalls in these areas. However, their behavior is consistent with global warming since precipitation is predicted to increase in high northern and southern latitudes.

The present cycle of glacier recession has, to a large extent, been a direct response to the ending of the Little Ice Age and the onset of a natural cycle of global warming, particularly in the first part of the twentieth century. However, emissions of greenhouse gases from the burning of fossil fuels and land-use changes are now believed to be contributing significantly to the current phase of warming. If the predictions of continued global warming are borne out, it seems likely that many glaciers will disappear and that only remnants of the larger and higher mountain glaciers will survive into the twenty-second century. However, such glaciers have advanced and retreated in the past. Some even disappeared during a period of warmer climates 5000 years ago, but then re-formed as the climate subsequently became colder. What is different today is that human activity, through the emissions of greenhouse gases, is now

*Glacier Bay National Park, Alaska, is a prime destination for glacier
sight-seeing cruises. Lamplugh Glacier provides a spectacular backdrop.*

believed to be driving global warming, and glacier changes in some parts of the world could start to exceed those that occurred earlier in the present interglacial (the last 11,500 years).

Further recession of mountain glaciers will have a number of effects. First, about one-third of the average predicted rise in global sea level of 1.6 feet (0.5 meters) by the end of the present century is predicted to come from the melting of mountain glaciers. Second, there will be effects on water resources. Increased glacier melting will probably increase water availability for a time, possibly increasing flood risks, but as glaciers start to disappear, the long-term forecast is for decreasing water supplies in those areas dependent on glacier sources. Third, steep moraine slopes are likely to be unstable for a time after they have been abandoned by the glaciers, and as more water is added to moraine-dammed lakes, the potential for glacier lake outbursts will remain high. Fourth, mountain tourism may be affected as the visual appeal of some regions diminishes without the presence of glaciers or the summer snowfields they provide for skiing.

Ice Sheets and Ice Shelves

Because of their vast size and remoteness, it has been difficult until recently to assess the state of health of the Greenland and Antarctic ice sheets. However, the application of new measurement techniques from aircraft and satellites is starting to allow changes in the ice surface altitudes to be estimated. For Greenland, the initial conclusions are that the higher central parts of the ice sheet are relatively stable, whereas at lower elevations the ice is getting thinner. The Antarctic ice sheet appears to be more or less in balance. Predictions of increased precipitation at higher latitudes mean that the Antarctic ice sheet may actually increase in size, but in Greenland, any increased snow accumulation may be offset by greater melting.

Following the disintegration of the ice shelves on the northern Antarctic Peninsula, concerns have been voiced in the media about the stability of the vast Ross and Filchner-

Mount Fairweather and Grand Plateau Glacier, Alaska.

Ronne ice shelves that border the West Antarctic ice sheet. The loss of these ice shelves could make the ice sheet itself more vulnerable to accelerated recession. However, there is no indication that these large ice shelves are threatened. They are located much further south than those on the Antarctic Peninsula and where the climate is much colder.

Moreover, the climate warming on the Antarctic Peninsula is not happening elsewhere in Antarctica, far less on the scale required to place them at risk – for this to happen, the climate would need to warm by some 18°F (10°C). The loss of the ice shelves on the northern Antarctic Peninsula is no more than a measure of regional warming in a small part of Antarctica.

Polar ice tongue, Antarctica.

As far as the long-term stability of the West Antarctic ice sheet is concerned, the jury is still out. If the grounding lines of the fast ice streams that drain the ice sheet were to retreat unchecked, this could lead to rapid disintegration of the ice sheet since much of it lies grounded below sea level. If it has collapsed in the past, as some evidence suggests, then clearly it could do so again. It is also uncertain whether the ice sheet has yet receded to its full interglacial minimum extent because of the time lag in its response to warming thousands of years ago. The probability is that it is relatively stable and unlikely to collapse drastically in the next few centuries. However, it may continue to shrink further as part of its response to the climate warming at the start of the present interglacial, or if the present interglacial is significantly prolonged by global warming. The much larger East Antarctic ice sheet is considered to be stable and may even increase in size because of increased snowfall.

While much attention has focused on the stability of the West Antarctic ice sheet, the Greenland ice sheet should not be overlooked. There is now evidence that much, or all, of it may have melted in the past and contributed significantly to the higher sea levels recorded in previous interglacials. Because its bed is above present sea level, unlike the West Antarctic ice sheet, its response to global warming is likely to be less drastic than disintegration of the West Antarctic ice sheet would be. Nevertheless, its complete melting could raise world sea level by some 23 feet (7 meters) and have a huge effect on coastal geography and societies. A temperature rise of about 9-14°F (5-8°C) would be required for this to happen. Such an increase lies at the upper end of the latest 'worst case' predictions for the end of the twenty-first century. However, even partial melting could have significant effects.

Some mountain glaciers may disappear as a result of global warming.

In view of the prediction of continued global warming due to increased concentrations of greenhouse gases in the atmosphere from human activities, the most likely scenario is one of continued glacier recession and disappearance of small mountain glaciers during the twenty-first century. However, due to the natural variability of the climate, there are likely to be cooler intervals when glacier recession may be temporarily interrupted in some parts of the world. In the longer term, predictions suggest that the climate downturn into the next widespread glaciation will not be averted by global warming, although it will be delayed.

A world of ice, Transantarctic Mountains, Victoria Land, Antarctica.

Index

*Entries in **bold** indicate pictures*

Further Reading

Alley, R. B., *The Two-Mile Time Machine*. Princeton University Press, 2000.

Andersen, B. G., & Borns Jr., H. W., *The Ice Age World*. 2nd edition, Scandinavian University Press, 1997.

Benn, D. I., & Evans, D. J. A., *Glaciers and Glaciation*. Arnold, 1998.

Hambrey, M., & Alean, J., *Glaciers*. Cambridge University Press, 1992.

Post, A., & La Chapelle, E. R., *Glacier Ice*. University of Washington Press, 2000.

Sharp, R., *Living Ice: Understanding Glaciers and Glaciation*. Cambridge University Press, 1988.

Biographical Note & Acknowledgements

John Gordon is the Earth Science Group Manager at Scottish Natural Heritage. A member of the International Glaciological Society, he has studied and visited glaciers all over the world. Early in his career, John studied glacial landforms and landscapes in Scotland, but later moved on to glaciers when he fell under the spell of the Antarctic and Arctic. John has published numerous academic journal articles and books on glaciers and glacial landforms. He lives in East Lothian, Scotland.

He thanks Mike Bentley and Neil Glasser for comments on the text.